P9-CCM-793

Brian
Bassyle

PUZZLE DUNGEON

Susannah Leigh
Illustrated by Brenda Haw

Layout by Nick Stone

Contents

Series Editor: Gaby Waters
Assistant Editor: Michelle Bates

About this book

This book is about Carla, her cat Ginger and their adventures in Puzzle Dungeon. There is a puzzle on every double page. See if you can solve them all. If you get stuck, you can look at the answers on pages 31 and 32.

Puzzle Dungeon is dark and mysterious and lies deep underground. It's not far away, but Carla doesn't know anyone who has ever been there before. Until now that is . . .

This is Carla's cat, Ginger

This is Carla

. . . Carla has just had a letter from her best friend, Billy. Billy wants to be an inventor when he grows up. He has gone down to Puzzle Dungeon to try out his latest experiment. Read his letter to find out more.

This is Billy

early morning

Dear Carla

I am going down to Puzzle Dungeon to test out my latest invention – some bright green glow-in-the-dark paint! (Puzzle Dungeon is the darkest place I can think of).

I promise to be back at 2 o'clock this afternoon to tell you all about my adventures.

Love Billy

Carla was worried by the letter. She had heard some very spooky stories about Puzzle Dungeon. Spiders as big as houses, scary monsters and deadly snakes were said to live there. Billy was very brave to go down on his own. Carla hoped he would be all right.

2

Things to spot

Billy might be brave, but he is also very good at losing things. You will find something he has dropped on almost every double page, starting on pages 6-7. You can see a picture of all the things to look out for here.

bandage

paintbrush

jumping frog

comic book

toffee

inventor's goggles

chewing gum

can of paint

little purse

test tube

teddy

Skeleton Sid

Sid the skeleton lives in Puzzle Dungeon. Look out for him on almost every double page. Don't worry, he is quite friendly – but a little shy.

You'll only find me in the dungeon, so start looking on page 8.

Dungeon Beetles

Watch out for the flying beetles who live in Puzzle Dungeon. You will find them on almost every double page.

You'll only find us in the dungeon!

Billy is late

It was 3 o'clock. Billy had said he would be back at two, but there was still no sign of him. Carla was worried. Billy was good at losing things. What if he had lost himself in Puzzle Dungeon? There was only one thing to do. She would have to go and find him.

Carla thought hard. If she was going to a dungeon, she would need some dungeon equipment. She decided to take her bright green backpack, a bar of chocolate, her hat with the lamp on top, her jester's stick, a penguin mirror and a yellow handkerchief. But where were they all?

Can you find them?

Cousin Sophie

Poppy My Friend

Billy and his Parents

ATLAS

Which way?

Carla gathered up her equipment and set off. Puzzle Dungeon lay deep underground beneath a ruined castle, a short way from her village.

Carla knew that the only way into Puzzle Dungeon was through a little doorway in the hillside, but when she arrived, she saw lots of little doorways. Which one led to Puzzle Dungeon?

Start looking for Billy's things!

Then Carla remembered something. An old tale said that the door to Puzzle Dungeon was directly underneath an apple tree, and that five blue and five yellow flowers always bloomed around it. Carla looked closely at the doors and saw that the old tale was true. Now she knew which one to go through.

Which door leads to Puzzle Dungeon?

Underground!

Carla slowly pushed open the rusty door. She shone her light into the darkness and gulped nervously. She felt rather scared, but Billy was her best friend and she had to find him. She couldn't turn back now.

With Ginger following close behind, Carla began the journey deep down into the mysterious underground world of Puzzle Dungeon . . .

First they crawled along a passage.

The earth was crumbly and cold.

Suddenly the passage turned into a deep hole.

There were hand and footholds, but it was still very scary.

They climbed down a ladder and reached the bottom of the hole. In the gloom, Carla saw a large cave, with five doors leading from it. She groaned. More doors!

As she looked around she saw something that made her think Billy had been here before. Now she knew which way he had gone.

Now you are in the dungeon, so watch out for us and Sid.

Which way should she go to follow Billy?

9

Creepy cavern

Carla followed the fluorescent footprints through the door. Then they disappeared. Billy's paint wasn't working very well!

Carla stopped short. She was in a deep cavern filled with thick green slime. On the other side was an archway. It was the start of another path, and it seemed to be the only way to go next. But to get to it, she would have to cross the cavern.

To cross the cavern, use the giant pillars as stepping stones. Do not step on the star shaped pillars. They will give you itchy feet and a spotty rash!

Then Carla saw a notice. She read it carefully and looked back at the cavern. She saw the giant pillars rising from the slime. The way looked easy enough. Carla wondered if Billy had already gone across. She hoped he hadn't fallen in. Carla would do what the notice said, being very careful where she stepped.

Can you find the safe way across the pillars?

Dungeon prisoners

Carla jumped off the last pillar and ran through the archway into a crumbling stone chamber. Iron rings hung from the walls, and ropes lay on the ground.

"This must have been where the dungeon prisoners were kept," Carla shuddered.

There was no way out apart from back the way they'd come. Or was there? As Carla read the carvings on the walls, she saw that one of them held a back to front clue. There was another way out of the chamber after all!

How can they get out of the chamber?

Scary monsters

Carla pulled the ring and the secret door swung open. She stepped through it and almost jumped out of her skin. Giants and ogres, mummies and monsters stared back at her! But when she looked closer, she saw they were only statues.

Carla breathed a sigh of relief, when suddenly she noticed something else that made her jump. Was it her imagination, or was she being watched? Not by the unblinking eyes of the statues, but by some smaller creatures peering out from them.

How many of these creatures can you see?

Picture map

Four little creatures jumped out from their hiding places and said they were dungeon dwellers. They were quite friendly. What's more, they had seen Billy.

They showed Carla a map and tried to tell her where Billy had gone next. But they all had different ideas. Carla was confused. They couldn't all be right. She looked at the map and realized only one suggestion fitted the pictures exactly. This was where Billy had gone.

Can you see which suggestion fits the picture map?

We live in Puzzle Dungeon and make things out of metal.

We've already seen Billy. We'll try to help you find him.

I think Billy went to the bats' nest beside the yellow rocks.

Map Key:

⭐ You are h

▬ Dead en

I'm sure it was the creepy crypt he was looking for, next to the bone heap.

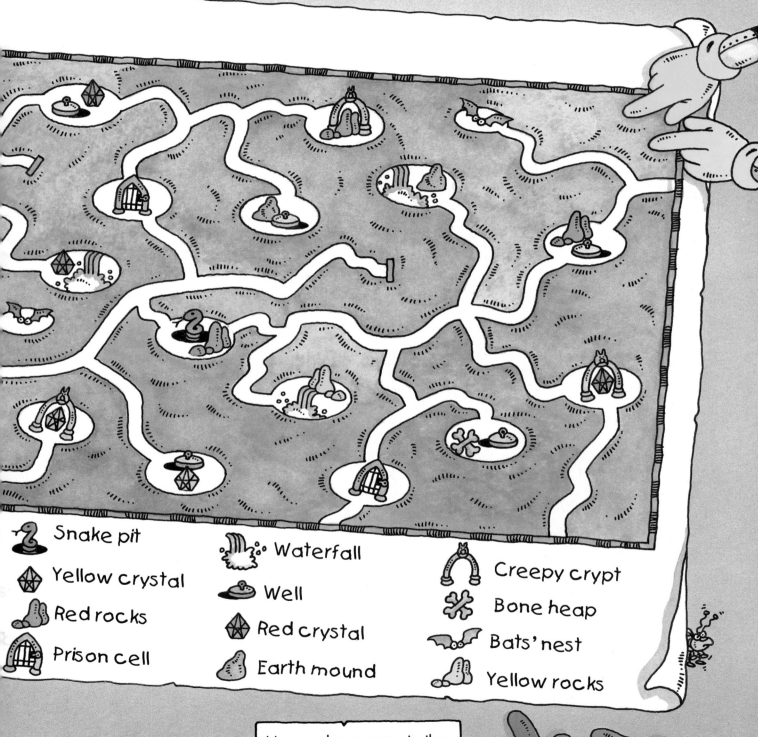

Perhaps he went to look at the yellow crystal at the waterfall.

🐍 Snake pit

◈ Yellow crystal

🪨 Red rocks

🚪 Prison cell

💧 Waterfall

⬤ Well

◈ Red crystal

🪨 Earth mound

⌂ Creepy crypt

✾ Bone heap

🦇 Bats' nest

🪨 Yellow rocks

He may have gone to the well, next to the red rocks.

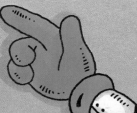

Hungry snakes

Carla set off for the well with her new friends. But just before they turned a corner, the dungeon dwellers stopped.

"We don't dare go any further, Carla," they said. "There are poisonous snakes near here. You are taller and braver than us. If you can find a plain green mushroom for each snake to eat, you can pass them safely."

Can you find the green mushrooms? You will need one for each snake.

FAKE SNAKE

LAUNDRY BASKET

Mouse trouble

Carla and Ginger the cat left the chomping snakes and hurried on their way. Soon they came to the room where the well was supposed to be, but there was no sign of it. All Carla could see were mice, playing in the room. They looked as if they were having fun. Carla stood in the doorway wondering what to do next, when she was startled by a loud MEOW from Ginger.

Ginger pounced into the room, and in a flash he had chased the mice away. Carla shook her head. She felt sorry for the mice. She wanted to tell them not to be scared. She knew Ginger wouldn't really hurt them. But now she couldn't see them anywhere.

Can you see where all the mice have gone? (Have you spotted the cover of the well?)

Spider's web

The mice weren't taking any chances with Ginger in the room, so they stayed well hidden.

Carla walked over to the well. Using her jester's stick, she levered off the cover. It slid away easily. Perhaps Billy had already been here . . . Carla peered into the inky blackness below. She couldn't give up her search now. The only way was down.

She saw what looked like a rope.

It was slightly sticky and a bit stretchy.

But it held her weight, so she climbed down.

As she climbed, she heard a voice from below.

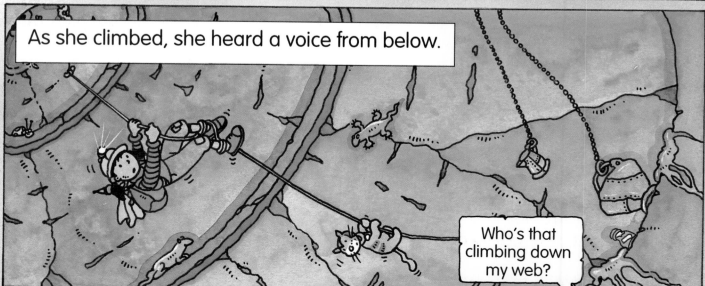

Who's that climbing down my web?

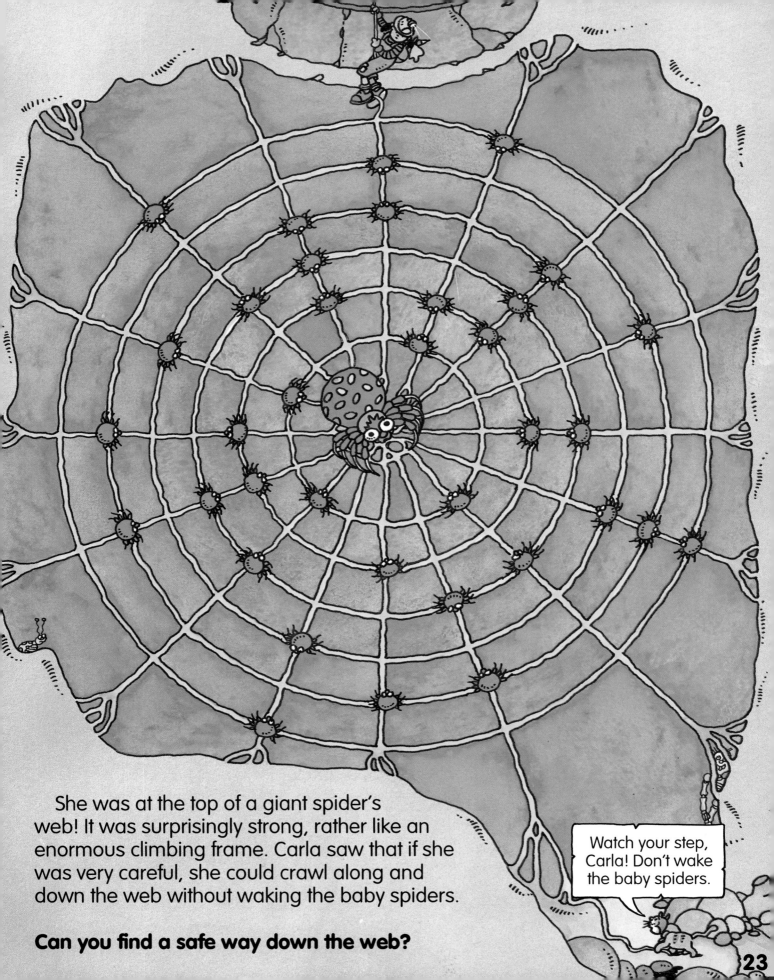

She was at the top of a giant spider's web! It was surprisingly strong, rather like an enormous climbing frame. Carla saw that if she was very careful, she could crawl along and down the web without waking the baby spiders.

Can you find a safe way down the web?

Watch your step, Carla! Don't wake the baby spiders.

Shiny cavern

Carla and Ginger scrambled safely down the web and through a stone archway. They were in a shimmery blue cave. Twinkling green lights sparkled all around. Carla looked closely and saw that the lights were glow worms. What's more, they seemed to be singing a strangely soothing song.

Then Carla saw Billy. He was sound asleep. She tried to call out to him, but she was feeling rather drowsy. From far away she heard a voice. It was Sid the skeleton! She had to do what he said, and fast.

Can you do what Sid says?

My turn to help has come at last.
You'll sleep as well, if you're not fast.
So find the magic flask-and-cup,
Give Billy a drink and he'll wake up.

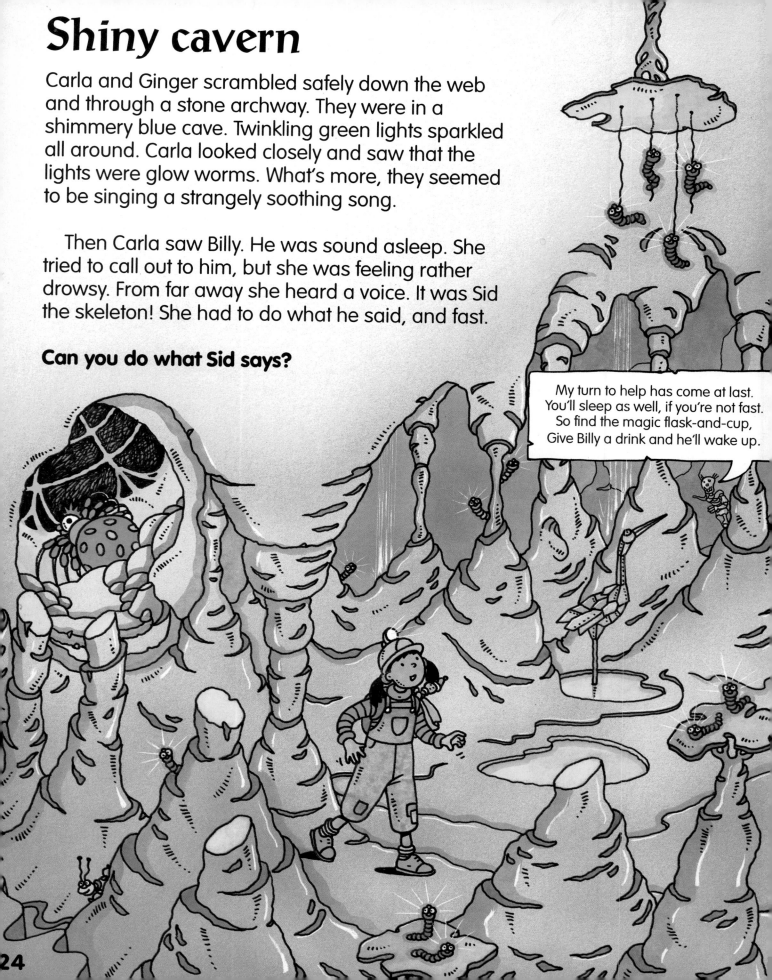

Secret lake

Carla took a sip from the magic cup. At once she felt wide awake. She poured some magic liquid into Billy's mouth. He woke up and rubbed his eyes. He was very surprised to see Carla.

"Did you see the glow worms, Carla?" he said. "They shine in the dark much better than my paint does."

"Let's go home," said Carla. "It's getting late."

But going back the same way meant . . .

Suddenly, Ginger darted off through a small hole in between some rocks.

"Come back Ginger!" Carla called.

But Ginger had disappeared.

"We'll have to go and find him," said Carla. "We can't leave him here. Who knows what could happen to him?"

They followed Ginger through the hole and found themselves on the shore of an underground lake. Light from a raised portcullis streamed across the water. Maybe there was another way out of the dungeon! They could use a boat to get across the water, but they didn't all look very safe.

Which boat do you think they should use?

Home at last!

They jumped into the little boat, pedalled through the open portcullis and out of Puzzle Dungeon. They blinked their eyes in the bright sunshine and saw they were in the middle of a lake. People were standing on the shore.

"Where are we?" asked Billy, still groggy from sleep.

Carla knew exactly where they were, and what's more, she could see some very familiar faces.

Do you know where they are, and do you recognize some of the people here?

That evening

Later that evening, Billy and Carla sat sipping cocoa at Carla's house. As they sat, they talked about their adventures in Puzzle Dungeon.

"I think I'll be testing my inventions above ground from now on," said Billy. "Puzzle Dungeon is a bit scary for me."

Ginger purred sleepily and dreamed about the dungeon dwellers. What funny creatures they were, and what strange metal objects they had made.

Look back through the book again. What do you think the dungeon dwellers might have made?

Answers

Pages 4-5 Billy is late

The six pieces of dungeon equipment are circled here.

Pages 6-7 Which Way?

This door leads to Puzzle Dungeon.

Pages 8-9 Underground!

Carla should follow Billy through this door. She has seen some of his green glow-in-the dark paint.

Pages 10-11 Creepy cavern

The safe way across the pillars is marked in red.

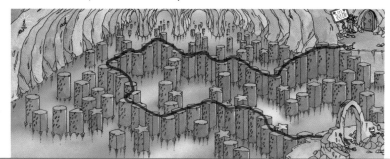

Pages 12-13 Dungeon prisoners

They can get out of the chamber by reading this message in mirror writing and doing what it says.

Here is what the message says the right way around:
Find a ring that looks like this. Pull it and a secret door will open.

Here is the ring they must pull.

Pages 14-15 Scary monsters

There are four little creatures. They are circled here.

Pages 16-17 Picture map

Billy has gone to the well next to the red rocks. This is the only place that is really on the map. All the other suggestions don't match up.

Pages 18-19 Hungry snakes

The green mushrooms are circled here. There are ten, one for each snake.

Pages 20-21
Mouse trouble

The mice are hiding. Their tails are circled here.

This is cover of the well.

Pages 22-23
Spider's web

The safe way down the web is marked in black.

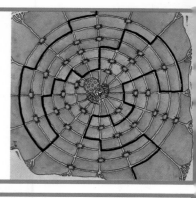

Pages 24-25
Shiny cavern

Sid tells Carla to look for the magic flask-and-cup. They are here.

Pages 26-27
Secret lake

They should use this boat. It is the safest.

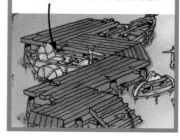

Pages 28-29 Home at last!

They are at the lake in their village. (You have seen a picture of it on page 6). Carla can see her parents, and Billy's parents. (You can see pictures of them on pages 4-5).

Carla's parents are circled in red. Billy's parents are circled in black.

Did you spot everything?
Dungeon beetles

Did you remember to count the dungeon beetles and find one of Billy's things on almost every double dungeon page? The chart below tells you where to find everything.

Billy's things

Sid the skeleton

Did you spot Sid the skeleton down in Puzzle Dungeon? He enjoyed watching Carla's dungeon journey, and he was happy to help at the end!

Pages	Beetles	Billy's things
6-7	none	little purse
8-9	two	bandage
10-11	two	test tube
12-13	three	comic book
14-15	four	toffee
16-17	three	inventor's goggles
18-19	three	chewing gum
20-21	three	paint brush
22-23	three	can of paint
24-25	two	teddy bear
26-27	three	jumping frog
28-29	none	none

This edition first published in 2003 by Usborne Publishing Ltd., Usborne House, 83-85 Saffron Hill, London EC1N 8RT, England.

www.usborne.com Copyright © 2003, 1994 Usborne Publishing Ltd.

U.E. Printed in Portugal.

First Published in America March 1995.